Original title:
Life's Meaning Is in the Details… Or Is It?

Copyright © 2025 Creative Arts Management OÜ
All rights reserved.

Author: Oliver Bennett
ISBN HARDBACK: 978-1-80566-110-8
ISBN PAPERBACK: 978-1-80566-405-5

Serenity in Seconds

Sunshine spills on morning toast,
A dancing crumb, my breakfast host.
I search for meaning in the jam,
Must I ponder or just eat, ma'am?

Forget the grand and lofty thoughts,
A sock with holes, how time begot.
The vacuum roars, but what's the fuss?
I hear it sing, it's part of us.

A chair that squeaks, a cat that trills,
The silly dance of daily thrills.
Do I find truth in avocado?
Or simply grin, then call it bravado?

With every sip from my cup of tea,
The world spins on, quite joyfully.
In tiny moments, we discover,
The quirky charm life can uncover.

Whispers of Wonder

In shadows cast by kitchen light,
A missing spoon gives way to fright.
Where did it go, I raise my brow,
Oh, steal my heart, you sneaky cow!

A potted plant that sports a face,
It winks at me with such great grace.
I ponder deep, what does it see?
A leaf or two, or just me?

The distant sound of playful barks,
Chasing squirrels through snowy parks.
What lesson here? Just chase, they say,
Until you trip, then find your way.

The clock strikes twelve, it's time for pie,
Each slice a secret, oh me, oh my!
In crumbs and laughs, I find delight,
In simple joys, my heart takes flight.

Threads of Tomorrow

In the weave of daily tasks,
We find patterns, not mere masks.
A sock's missing, it makes us grin,
It's a tale of triumph, or our sin.

A spoon that dances on the plate,
Reminds us of our quirky fate.
The cat's asleep, dreaming so bold,
While we chase moments, silver and gold.

The Quiet Moments

A sip of coffee, the world anew,
The silence speaks, in shades of blue.
A ladybug on the window pane,
Winks at me, as if to explain.

The tick of clocks, a rhythmic beat,
Pants the dogs in summer heat.
A squirrel flips, oh what a show,
As if he knows more than we know.

In the Corners of the Ordinary

Dust bunnies spin tales as they roam,
Underneath furniture that feels like home.
A pizza slice left on the floor,
Is tomorrow's snack, who could ask for more?

Leftover stories in the fridge,
Haunt the midnight dreams we bridge.
Chairs that creak, with laughter's tune,
Whisper secrets under the moon.

Marvels in the Margins

In the margins of our busy days,
Lies the laughter in strange ways.
A fly that buzzes with a grin,
Buzzing truths hidden within.

A crooked picture upon the wall,
Holds memories that gently call.
The crumbs on the table tell a tale,
Of feasts and friends that never pale.

Crumbs of Reflection

In the crumbs of toast we ponder,
A universe of breakfast blunders.
The jam's a mess, yet we all laugh,
Is this the secret? A sticky path.

The coffee spills, a bitter dance,
With splashes bright, we take a chance.
In chaos found, a spark ignites,
Is that where joy in mornings bites?

The Clock Ticks Softly

Tick-tock says the clock, nonchalant,
While we debate if this all counts.
Time winks with a playful grin,
Reminding us where laughter's been.

Seconds scoff at grand designs,
As quirky thoughts weave through the lines.
The hands race on, with no regret,
Why fix the clock if it's a pet?

Daydreams and Detritus

Beneath my desk, the wrappers lie,
They hold my dreams and late-night snacks' high.
Each crumpled piece, a story told,
The meaning found, or so I'm sold.

A dusty lamp lights up my mind,
While daydreams dance, both sweet and blind.
The mundane spark ignites the fun,
In cluttered spaces, chaos won.

A Whispering Universe

In whispers soft, the cosmos sighs,
Each twinkle hides a small surprise.
Stars chuckle down, they treat us well,
In tiny tales where giggles dwell.

The breeze is full of goofy chatter,
Like socks lost in the big wash scatter.
Do planets laugh at our dismay?
Or keep our secrets 'til the day?

Whispers from the Unremarkable

In the corner, a sock but one,
A missing pair, it's kind of fun!
A lone shoe dances, it knows the beat,
With twists and turns, it's life's small treat.

The crumbs on the table, a feast of delight,
They sing their tales in the morning light.
A cup half full, or is it half gone?
Does it matter if the coffee's on?

Small Things Matter

A pebble on the path, oh what a find!
It's smoother than glass, a treasure unlined.
In the fridge, a jar of mustard glows,
A party of sandwiches, nobody knows.

The cat on the window, judging the day,
Chasing dust motes in her haughty ballet.
A sneaky fly lands on the cake with glee,
It's an uninvited guest, can't you see?

Artistry in the Everyday

A toast to the dishes in the sink piled high,
   A modern art piece, oh me, oh my!
With spatters of sauce, a culinary smudge,
   Who needs a gallery? Let's not judge!

The occasional sock that decided to roam,
   Wanders the house, it's far from home.
In the chaos, a beauty, unnoticed, it's true,
   Each tiny detail bursting with hue!

Cracks in the Facade

A tiny crack in the kitchen tile,
A grand reminder to stop, pause, and smile.
It tells a story of wear and of tear,
Embrace the chaos, there's charm everywhere!

The dust bunnies dance under the bed,
Hosting a party, they laughed and they fed.
While we chase after dreams, big and bold,
The little things whisper, their secrets untold.

Little Wonders

A bug lands on my sandwich,
It makes a little dance,
I watch it with my fingers,
As if this was my chance.

The crumbs spread like confetti,
A feast for ants nearby,
They march in straight formation,
And I just wave goodbye.

The sun is shining brightly,
But my drink has lost its fizz,
I search for hidden treasures,
Like finding gold in whiz.

Some moments seem so silly,
Like socks that mix and clash,
Yet in this maze of nonsense,
I find my heart's sweet stash.

Handfuls of Solitude

In my room, a quiet mouse,
It steals a slice of cheese,
I wonder if it's happy,
Or if it just likes ease.

A potted plant is blooming,
It's growing a bit weird,
I swear it's out to get me,
It stares and looks so leered.

The clock is ticking loudly,
I check how time can crawl,
It counts the hours slowly,
Yet I just binge it all.

With cookies in the oven,
I forget the drying load,
The laundry's now a mountain,
But cookies are my road.

Flecks of Joy

A rainbow in my cereal,
I munch with glee galore,
Each color brings a giggle,
I always crave some more.

A sneeze that comes unexpected,
It echoes down the hall,
I scaring all the pigeons,
As they flee from my brawl.

The cat jumps on the counter,
It thinks it's quite the star,
With paws in every cupcake,
It dreams of being far.

The laughter in the bubbles,
As I soak in my retreat,
Each splash is pure giggles,
Who knew that fun's so sweet?

The Subtle Symphony

The clatter of the dishes,
As forks take their own flight,
I laugh at dinner's chaos,
It's music in the night.

My pants are dancing wildly,
They've shrunk a little tight,
I wiggle like a mute fish,
Now who's holding on right?

A sneeze spills forth a giggle,
With friends, we burst in tears,
The best part of the evening,
Is sharing all our fears.

A toast to little blunders,
With drinks that spill and sway,
In every awkward moment,
There's a tune we must play.

Elegance in Simplicity

A noodle bends, a shoe untied,
A whispered joke, a cat that sighed.
We chase our tails, we trip and fall,
But hey, that's part of the ball!

An unkempt lawn, a pot that's cracked,
The ripest fruit, unkindly snacked.
With quirky quirks, we dance and flip,
Embrace the mess, it's all a trip!

A mismatched sock, a worn-out chair,
Hiding treasures in the air.
Between the lines, delight awaits,
In silly snafus, laughter rates!

So grab your cake, and raise a cheer,
For joyful chaos, we hold dear.
In simple things, we find our song,
In life's blunders, we all belong!

Hidden Treasures

A tattered map, a fortune's grace,
In grandma's attic, quite the space.
The jars of buttons, dust, and threads,
Are gems we treasure in our heads!

We sift through piles, in search of gold,
A mystery box of joys untold.
With every find, we laugh and tease,
Unraveling life, with such unease!

A mismatched toy, a note from school,
These hidden gems, our heart's own fuel.
In every nook, a tale's begun,
In silly spots, we find our fun!

So let's embark, with bags in hand,
Explore the chaos, oh so grand.
For treasures lie in strange places,
In giggles, jokes, and silly faces!

The Silence in Between

The quiet pause, the awkward glance,
In jumbled thoughts, we lose our chance.
But in the stillness, sparkles flick,
A chuckle stirs; oh, what a trick!

We grasp at words, they slip away,
In silent moments, laughter play.
The know-it-alls, they think they're wise,
But chuckling at those silly tries!

An empty room, a lingering beat,
Where absent minds and giggles meet.
The pauses hold a messy grace,
In awkward moments, we find our place!

So revel in the hush and cheer,
In every blank, there's fun to steer.
With no regrets, we leap and bound,
In silent joys, our laughs resound!

Glimmers of Truth

A half-baked thought, a jest or two,
That flower pot, it's cracked right through.
In silly slips, we seek the light,
Let's dance around the truth tonight!

With quirky lines, we weave our tale,
The twists and turns, they never fail.
In goofy claims and bold debates,
We often find what laughter rates!

A glimmer sparkles in our eyes,
As nonsense leads to sweet surprise.
In chasing facts, we trip or tangle,
But that's the joy—let's take a wrangle!

So lift your glass and toast the laughs,
To all the quirks and silly crafts.
With truth in jest, we roam and play,
In life's grand mix, we find our way!

Droplets of Meaning

In the morning, toast burns with flair,
A dance of crumbs flies through the air.
Butter glides, a slippery slide,
While coffee leaps, a caffeinated tide.

A cat's meow, a sly little plot,
Turns serious talks to a giggly spot.
Among lost socks, a find that's rare,
A lonely spoon grins, in despair!

Fleeting Frames

Snapshots captured, a blink and they pass,
A face full of whipped cream, cheers with a glass.
Laughter erupts, oh, what a sight,
As the dog steals the cake, a glorious bite!

Chasing sunsets with rubbery shoes,
We scribble on napkins, share silly views.
Time flies faster than we can recall,
Sometimes it's just a myth, after all!

Threads of Memory

A threadbare sweater from the kind-heart seam,
Holds stories and laughter, like a happy dream.
As the buttons poke, we scratch our head,
Pondering the wisdom of things we've said.

Do socks hold secrets, or is it just us?
Each wrinkle and fold, a funny old fuss.
When bananas dance and the forks come alive,
Banishing worries, we somehow thrive!

The Secret in the Shadows

In the corner sits a dusty old shoe,
Whispering tales, if only we knew.
A sock puppet chorus, they lead us astray,
As the fridge hums a secret ballet!

The crumbs on the counter must hold a clue,
To mystery meals or a midnight stew.
When the clock chimes with a playful ring,
We dance with shadows, let laughter take wing!

The Unseen Heartbeat

In a world where socks are lost,
I find joy in the smallest cost.
A crunch of leaves beneath my feet,
Or a midday snack that can't be beat.

Butterflies dance, but who can see?
Are they laughing just like me?
I chase the shadow of my dreams,
While sipping lemonade by the streams.

The cat approves of my weird hat,
And winks at all the thoughts I chat.
In the kitchen, burnt toast sings,
With every flop, new laughter springs.

So raise your glass to silly things,
The joy that even chaos brings.
In every glitch and twist of fate,
There lies a giggle, small yet great.

Layers of Luminosity

The sun sets with a comic flair,
Painting skies with colors rare.
A bubblegum pink, quite absurd,
Makes me laugh in the twilight blurred.

I swear I saw a squirrel in shorts,
Giving me fashion thoughts of sorts.
He twirled around with daring grace,
Prompting giggles on my face.

In every grain of sand I find,
The secrets of a giggling mind.
The ocean waves wink with delight,
As I squish my toes, oh what a sight!

So let's toast to the zany shows,
To silly sparkles that life bestows.
For in the chaos, joy does bloom,
In every corner, find the room.

The Quiet Canvas

On a canvas that whispers dreams,
I stomp through puddles, hear the gleams.
A messy paint of life so bright,
Makes me chuckle with sheer delight.

With every dribble, splat, and smear,
The artwork hums a tune so clear.
But wait! A brush stole my last snack,
As I stared, the dog gave me a smack.

The quiet moments can truly shout,
As I wrestle with a sleepy clout.
The cat claims my chair, full of pride,
While I sit tangled in dreams wide.

So here's to chaos that brings a grin,
To doodles where the fun begins.
In every scribble, laughter swells,
In the portrait of life, humor dwells.

Tones of Tranquility

I sip my tea, a moment divine,
But oh! Look at that cat on the line!
An acrobat on a fence so high,
As I chuckle, he waves goodbye.

In the garden, weeds play a tune,
Dancing along to the sun's monsoon.
I try to prune, but they just laugh,
Unruly souls on a botanical path.

Clouds wear hats that float up high,
Winking at birds as they swoop by.
Each tiny detail whispers cheer,
In the quiet, silliness is near.

So let's revel in the quirks we find,
In the smallest moments, so aligned.
For in the odd, sweet truth resides,
And joy will follow as laughter glides.

The Little Things That Linger

A crumb on the floor, a sock in the sink,
The mysteries abound, they make you think.
Forgotten leftovers, a shoelace astray,
They whisper their secrets in a curious way.

A scratch on the wall, an old faded book,
Beneath all those layers, just take a look.
The chaos around us, a treasure chest,
Where laughter hides deep, life's quirky quest.

Layers of Perception

A cup half-empty, coffee gone cold,
Do we see the glass, or tales left untold?
A rainy day's joy, a puddle to splash,
Or the gray clouds looming, we tend to clash.

A neighbor's loud music, a reason to dance,
In odd little moments, we find our chance.
Peering through glasses, in thick frames of thought,
We laugh at the small things that life has brought.

Serendipity in Silence

A cat on the roof, with the sun in its eyes,
Sipping on calmness, no need for a prize.
The world spins around, a silent ballet,
Where whispers of chaos dream light-years away.

A traffic jam waits, a snail's paced parade,
Yet jazz tunes emerge, in the noise they wade.
Each honk like a note, each sigh a soft beat,
In still, funny moments, we find our sweet seat.

Clarity in Chaos

A soup of confusion, ingredients wild,
Yet somewhere within, lies the heart of a child.
The socks that don't match, they giggle and tease,
In chaos we find what it means to be free.

A party of thoughts, like a jumbled display,
Yet laughter erupts in a most unexpected way.
The jokes that we share, the quirks that we find,
In the mad swirl of life, we're perfectly blind.

Fragments of Existence

In the morning, toast burns bright,
Coffee spills, but what a sight!
Cats knock things off, a clumsy show,
While I chase crumbs, they steal the dough.

Neighbors yell, your lawn's a mess,
But I'm just here for the Sunday dress.
Birds chirp like they've got a plan,
While I wonder if I'm still a fan.

Laughter echoes, kids run wild,
Chasing bubbles, life's just a child.
With socks that don't match, I contemplate,
If it's fashion or fate? Oh, it's great!

Yet in the chaos, oh what a tease,
I find joy in the smallest ease.
Are these the fragments, bits of gold?
Or a jigsaw puzzle, too hard to hold?

The Subtle Symphony

In the kitchen, pots clang loud,
Cooking pasta, I feel so proud.
But a noodle's dance can cause a fright,
As my dog sighs; he wants a bite.

Then the doorbell rings, oh what a din,
Is it pizza or trouble knocking in?
I check my hair, it's standing tall,
And wonder if I should answer at all.

Dancing to music, socks a mismatch,
Wobbling like a funhouse, who'll dispatch?
Neighbors peeking, what's going down?
While I've spun myself into a clown.

Yet among the noise, there's a tune,
In every blunder, a sweet commune.
Between pot lids and my crazy flair,
Life plays on—a comical affair!

In Every Whisper, a Truth

In whispers soft, I hear the clock,
Counting all the laughs that mock.
Cats plotting schemes on the windowsill,
As I trip over the forgotten grill.

The toast is burnt, the eggs all run,
Yet breakfast smiles when stirred with fun.
Each spoonful serves a giggling fate,
The secret ingredient? It's never late!

Kids ask why, as curious as they are,
With questions like, "Is a hot dog a star?"
I ponder the meaning between every bite,
In this buffet of confusion, pure delight!

So here's to whispers, loud and clear,
In every chuckle, a joy appears.
Though the world spins with questions real,
The vibrant giggles, oh, they reveal!

Beneath the Surface

Beneath the waves, a fish once squeaked,
In search of salad—oh, how it peaked!
With bubbles forming, it made a plea,
"Where's the ranch dressing? Just let me be!"

In puddles deep, I saw a frog,
Wearing a crown; was it a bog?
Jumping high like it owned the place,
While I chuckled at its royal grace.

Clouds drift lazily, racing my thought,
Should I run in? Wait, what's it caught?
Every shadow dances, something's amiss,
Yet the sun peeks in, a playful kiss.

In every corner, fun must ensue,
Life's just silly, sprinkled with dew.
With each little quirk, lemons take flight,
Here's to giggles that shine in the night!

Threads of Thought

In the corner of my eye, a sock,
A pesky thread of fate, a flock.
Does it matter where it's gone?
Just a fluff by which we're drawn.

Chasing crumbs that lead to cheese,
Counting thoughts upon the breeze.
Perhaps a joke or two we see,
Or is it just the cat's decree?

Notes and doodles fill the page,
Where sanity meets a sage.
Is it deep or just absurd?
The answer's wrapped in a silly word.

So let's waltz to tunes unheard,
With quirks and giggles as the spur.
Each detail dances, spins, and flits,
A tapestry of zany bits.

Shadowed Realities

In shadows cast by frying pans,
We ponder deep and silly plans.
A salad toss, it's all a ruse,
Or is it life? Do we confuse?

The cat who sleeps without a care,
Knows more of bliss than I could dare.
With purrs and naps, the world's a game,
Each glance, a win, a roaring flame.

Where socks go missing, blame a ghost,
Or maybe it's the toaster's boast.
Last seen near a plate of fries,
Exploring truths disguised as lies.

Each shadow chuckles, pours a drink,
While I sit here and start to think.
A riddle wrapped in joyful haze,
The truth's a punchline in a maze.

The Fragility of Now

A fragile leaf dances on the air,
As whispers giggle and playfair.
The clock ticks loud, a mockery,
Of moments lost in laughter's spree.

Dishes pile high, a mountain peak,
Yet here I sit, too wise to speak.
"What's for dinner?" fate will tease,
Perhaps it's pizza, if you please!

Bubbles burst with stories old,
While life's absurd, yet still so bold.
In laughter's glow, we find our way,
A fragile hope in bright display.

So tiptoe through this funny dance,
Embrace the chaos; take a chance.
For in the mess, we find a rhyme,
And perhaps a reason wrapped in time.

Moments of Marvel

A sticky note, a quirky find,
Commands my brain, the ties that bind.
"Breathe," it says in crooked grace,
While I lose track of time and space.

Coffee spills, a masterpiece gone,
A canvas of chaos 'til the dawn.
Yet in this mess, a story brews,
Of laughter felt, of joyful hues.

The dog who thinks he owns the floor,
Strikes a pose by the open door.
Is he the king, the czar of glee?
Or just a pup who dreams to be?

So as we stumble, skip, and hop,
Let's raise a toast and never stop.
To moments small, to grand parade,
Where silly reigns, and joy's displayed.

Tiny Triumphs

A crumb found on the floor, oh what a delight,
It brings a grin—what a tiny bite.
The sock that's lost but now is found,
Such victories in the mundane abound.

The toast that pops with a joyful spring,
A moment to cherish, oh what a fling!
The parking spot right up at the front,
These little wins, we often flaunt.

A sneeze that's caught, a sip that's missed,
These simple things that can't be dismissed.
The joy of finding a missing pen,
These tiny triumphs make us grin again.

So laugh at the little while you can see,
In every stitch of life, a tiny glee.
With every bit of joy, we ignite our zest,
Finding triumphs in quirks, oh life is blessed!

Unraveled Mysteries

Where's the odd sock that disappeared?
It's a mystery that leaves us speared.
The cat in the box, with a curious stare,
Finding joy in stories that go nowhere.

A missing remote—where could it be?
Couch cushions hold secrets, oh so free.
The fridge holds treasures, a faded snack,
Ghosts from the past that we can't get back.

Why do we trip on the flat, even ground?
And why do lost keys seem to spy around?
Puzzle pieces of antics, they tickle our mind,
In the secrets of life, humor is what we find.

Oh, mysteries linger in laughter and light,
Chasing shadows in the day and the night.
We're detectives of joy, with a wink and a grin,
In every lost thing, new journeys begin!

Fragments of Time

A dropped ice cream, oh what a waste,
A childhood memory, so sweet, not to haste.
The time it rained while we danced in the sun,
Fragments of laughter, oh what fun!

The tick-tock of clocks that stop suddenly,
Bringing laughter from friends, it's quite funny.
The frozen moment when you trip and fall,
Life captures giggles, we cherish it all.

An awkward silence that stretches so wide,
Then bursts into laughter, with arms open wide.
Snapshots of blunders we carry with pride,
We weave these fragments, no need to hide.

So here's to the moments, both silly and sweet,
In fragments of time, our joys are complete.
For every tick and tock, let the fun unwind,
In the chaos of life, peace we will find!

The Delicate Balance

Balancing plates on a single stick,
One wrong move, and they tumble quick.
The art of pouring a drink too high,
A splash in the face? Oh me, oh my!

The dance with the dog as you weave through the room,
Careful not to stumble, or risk the vacuum's doom.
Juggling chores while avoiding the mess,
In delicate balancing, we find our success.

A fine line between chaos and calm,
Tickling the edges, like a soothing balm.
The trampoline jump that almost feels wrong,
Yet laughter erupts, like an upbeat song.

So laugh at the moments that dance through the air,
In the delicate balance, joy is laid bare.
Each little stumble, spills or spills just right,
Bring smiles into focus, as we dance through the night!

Mechanics of the Mundane

Woke up this morning, my sock's on the chair,
Did it leap? Or does it merely stare?
Forgot my coffee, oh the agony!
Can caffeine be an ungrateful deity?

A toaster's ambitions, just to make bread shine,
But crumbs conspire, oh what a design!
The fridge hums a tune, I swear it's a song,
Of leftovers pleading, 'Why must you be long?'

Each chair holds a secret, or maybe a snack,
Why do socks hide? They've plotted an act!
Dishes in towers, balancing with glee,
Are they training for some circus spree?

Oh, the wondrous world of the commonplace,
Where a lost spoon can start a whole chase.
Details laugh while we're busy, oh goodness!
Remind me again—was that a croissant or a mess?

Unfolding the Unnoticed

A tiny ant plays, like a general's plan,
Commanding the crumbs from my lunch, oh man!
While I'm distracted by the phone's bright screen,
He's plotting my downfall, crafty and mean.

A lightbulb flickers, like it knows a joke,
Do I fix it now, or just let it poke?
Mirrors reflect my sock's misaligned fate,
Twisting the thoughts of impending debate.

The calendar taunts, filled with things to do,
Did I really need to write 'Buy more glue?'
Dandelions pop through concrete with flair,
What's in a weed? A garden's despair?

Oh the beauty in chaos, chaos so fine,
Even a pigeon knows how to dine.
Take notes from the world, do they really care?
Sometimes a worm could be royalty somewhere!

The Depth of Dappled Light

Sunlight dances on leaves, a goofy ballet,
While squirrels critique, 'You're doing it wrong, stay!'
The shadows have secrets that tickle the ground,
In puddles, reflections, where nonsense is found.

A leaf flutters down, with dreams of a flight,
Landing by a cat, who's plotting tonight.
The bumblebee buzzes a rather loud tune,
To flowers that whisper, 'We've got to commune!'

The sun's lazy flicker, like it's lost in thought,
Sunburns the skin, man, I forgot what I bought!
A butterfly pauses, with a sassy flair,
Laughing at humans, standing unaware.

Here in the details, we find quirky delight,
In certain dull moments that sparkle so bright.
Oh the wonders we miss in the blinding glare,
While ants concoct plans—aware, oh so aware!

Petals on Pavement

Petals scatter like confetti from trees,
The sidewalk's a party, could it tease?
The wind whispers jokes, though it seldom will share,
With the curious cat, lounging without care.

Each passerby steps with a rhythm of grace,
Oblivious to nature's enchanting embrace.
A dog lifts a leg, not attending the show,
His majesty's ego can ruin the flow.

Oh how a raindrop can change the parade,
From sighs to squeaks, it's a slippery grade.
A squirrel steals blooms, plays the prankster of spring,
In gardens, the chaos wears laughter's bright ring.

So gather the details, though trivial they seem,
In the jokes of the universe, we're all in the meme.
Every tiny moment, a punchline in play,
In petals and puddles, life's comedy stays!

The Scent of the Mundane

In a cup of coffee, a dream might brew,
But spill it on a shirt, and you're feeling blue.
The laundry sings tales, of stubborn stains,
Adventures we have, in mundane chains.

A sock thrown out, on Tuesday's flight,
Reminds us of joy, in washing night.
A wrinkle here, a button there,
Finding you later, what a hilarious scare!

Inloaves of bread, crumbs dance with cheer,
Who knew the crust was a pioneer?
Jelly spills a secret, that time can mend,
Perhaps the fridge is a long-lost friend!

So raise a glass, to the socks that stray,
And the coffee that helps, come what may!
For in every spill, there's humor and glee,
Mundane magic, is joyful, you see!

Small Gestures, Grand Stories

A wave from a stranger, brightening your day,
A 'thank you' from the cashier, who knows the way.
In these tiny moments, giants reside,
With laughter and joy, they softly glide.

A smile in the mirror, while combing your hair,
Is like finding lost treasure, beyond compare.
The cat, with its antics, a whiskered delight,
Holds tales of mischief, that gleam in the night.

A forgotten birthday, who'd want a frown?
Yet cake in the fridge is the talk of the town!
A small birthday tune, off-key but sincere,
Brings a chorus of chuckles, and nothing to fear.

For in every blunder, lies a grand little tale,
Of laughter and joy, that never goes stale.
So cherish the quirky, the small and the bright,
In gestures so simple, discover pure light!

Echoes of the Infinite

The echo of laughter, in empty halls,
A bounce back of joy, with so many calls.
In a wink from a friend, in a silly dance,
Life winks back, asking for a chance.

Whispers in corners, where shadows play,
Tell stories of cats, who have gone astray.
A potted plant, an audience it keeps,
As it nods through the gossip, while the world sleeps.

The clock shares its tick-tock, chimes in delight,
As socks gossip secrets, of day turns to night.
A book on the shelf, that no one will read,
Contains a whole universe, waiting to heed.

In echoes we find, the dancing refrain,
Of moments that matter, sprinkle joy like rain.
So let laughter resound, like echoes of glee,
In the simple nonsense, we each can be free!

Insights in Simplicity

In a crumpled note, lies wisdom profound,
A doodled heart, that's artistically bound.
The world may chase grandeur, in glitter and gold,
Yet here, in the simple, true stories unfold.

A spilled bowl of cereal tells tales of a race,
The dog surfing crumbs, with such doggy grace.
The jigsaw unsolved, missing a piece,
Holds mysteries of fun, that never cease.

Two mugs, side by side, as dawn breaks anew,
Share whispers of friendship, over coffee so true.
A spoon sings old songs, of ice cream delight,
Of sprinkles and toppings, that dance in moonlight.

So find in simplicity, a grand little cheer,
In the twinkles and giggles, that life holds dear.
Let the quirks and the flaws, paint laughter in streaks,
For hidden in small things, are life's unique peaks!

Color in the Cracks

In a world of tiny bits,
We dance with whims and fits.
A broken vase, a pet's odd glare,
Sprinkle laughter everywhere.

A dusty book with pages torn,
Holds secrets of a time reborn.
A missing sock, a sock drawer war,
Who knew life had so much in store?

The sun sets low, the moon gives chase,
A lost remote, oh what a race!
Spilling coffee, choosing clothes,
Finding joy in all that shows.

With paint and laughter, mix the hues,
In silly moments, we can't lose.
So fill the cracks with every cheer,
For humor reigns, we hold it dear.

The Lingering Aftertaste

A sandwich gone a tad bit stale,
Leaves us laughing, what a tale!
When every bite's a gamble tossed,
The flavor lost, but joy's not cost.

A coffee spill, a gurgled slurp,
Add sweet mishaps to life's great perk.
For every meal, a laugh erupts,
In crumbs and quirks, we're surely cupped.

The spice of life, a pinch too weak,
Yet passionate dishes offer mystique.
With every sip, a story's spun,
And at the end, we laugh, it's fun!

So raise your glass, in jest we toast,
To every meal that offers most.
For in the taste, we find a jest,
And in the funny, we are blessed.

Hidden Harmonies

Upon this stage, we act in jest,
Finding rhythm in life's crazy quest.
A hiccup here, a tambourine there,
Life's symphony plays unaware.

The cat's meow like a trumpet blast,
Mismatched socks, but we hold fast.
In every clatter, a melody found,
Together we rise, together we sound.

The coffee pot sings a giddy tune,
A sock hop dance beneath the moon.
With every laugh, a chorus sings,
In subtle chaos, joy it brings.

So tune your heart to the silly beats,
Where quirk and charm make life complete.
In harmony, we lose the fuss,
And find the music in the bus!

Echoes of Essence

In whispers low, the echoes call,
A gushing laugh, we share it all.
A soggy shoe, a wobbly chair,
Essence of joy is everywhere.

The clock ticks loud, a metronome,
In every pause, we roam and comb.
A pebble toss, the splashy cheer,
With simple joys, we persevere.

Forgotten keys on the table lie,
While dancing shadows cast nearby.
In every chuckle, tales retold,
In echoes bright, our hearts behold.

So step right up, embrace the sound,
In quirky notes, our love is found.
The essence of here, a joyful spree,
In laughter's echo, forever free.

The Canvas of Ordinary

In a world of beige and brown,
The teapot's chipped, it wears a frown.
Yet in its cracks, a joke might lie,
A hidden tale, a silent sigh.

The paperclips dance, a wild show,
In the drawer where they often go.
They twirl and spin, a quirky crew,
Who knew office supplies had a view?

The socks that never seem to match,
Plotting schemes to cause a scratch.
In laundry piles, they plot and scheme,
A laugh, perhaps, a wink, a dream.

The latte art, a heart so bold,
Next to crumbs from tales retold.
In every sip, a giggle hides,
In frothy forms, life's joy abides.

Subtle Signs

A cloudless sky, yet rainboots worn,
The fish that swims, yet feels forlorn.
A banana peel, a classic slide,
Life's little tricks we cannot bide.

The cat in shades, a suave disguise,
With sleepy eyes that seem so wise.
He ponders life from window sills,
While plotting thoughts of gourmet meals.

The rogue sock greets each passerby,
A superhero in plain sight, oh my!
It tingles toes with mischief neat,
While cozy hands uphold defeat.

The clock ticks loud, with a smirk so sly,
It schemingly waves goodbye.
In every tick, a whispered jest,
Time tiptoes by, as if it's blessed.

Fleeting Glances

A moment lost in a glance or two,
The ice cream spills, a colorful hue.
A bike rides by, with squeaky charm,
And life's small mishaps do no harm.

The squirrel steals snacks, a daring thief,
Racing cars like a goofball chief.
In every nut, a treasure found,
The joyful jesters, all around.

A wink exchanged in crowded space,
The tip of hats, a quirky grace.
In oops and oohs, the laughter swells,
In those sweet moments, joy compels.

The flip-flops flop on sunny days,
Their rhythm set in silly ways.
In every step, a dance appears,
To celebrate our hopes and fears.

The Weight of Whimsy

The feather floats upon the breeze,
It tells a tale with such great ease.
Yet in its drift, a thought may spark,
A marshmallow fight awaits at dark.

The garden gnome, with mossy beard,
Stands guard for laughs when folks are leered.
In his stoic stance, he plots his fun,
A party under moonlight's run.

The fridge door squeaks, a secret shared,
While veggies gossip, slightly scared.
In every crunch, a whisper flows,
Of zany dreams a carrot knows.

The merry jingle from the ice cream van,
Inviting smiles, the joy of plan.
For in each bite of sprinkles bright,
Lies whimsy's weight, pure delight.

The Hidden Narratives

In a crumb on the carpet, a story resides,
A fairy tale lost where the breakfast abides.
The dog sniffs with wonder, the cat rolls her eyes,
What secrets are whispered beneath the pies?

Dust bunnies frolic, with dreams so bizarre,
Of traveling far in a toy car.
They plot with the spoons and the forks for their flight,
To a land where the cookies are baked every night.

A sock in the corner throws a wild rave,
Declaring that lost things will always misbehave.
Yet who needs a partner more stylish than this?
The quietest of chaos sometimes brings bliss.

In every small crack, a riddle will play,
Like the mysteries hiding in your tech's delay.
So pause for a moment and check what you've found,
The details are brighter when spun round and round.

Sipping Tea with Meaning

With a teacup in hand, I ponder and sip,
The bubbles keep rising, a whimsical trip.
Is steeping just water with dreams on the side?
Or a portal to wisdom where nonsense can hide?

My cat gives me judgment, she lives like a star,
While I chase after answers that never go far.
The cream swirls like thoughts in a fanciful dance,
Each sip a reminder of fate and chance.

The kettle whistles tales from the dark and the deep,
Of wisdom brewed slowly, but never to keep.
A bag of fine questions, steeped strong in my soul,
Could ponder the universe, or simply chew coal.

Yet as I sip slowly, I smile and I grin,
For all of this nonsense brings joy from within.
So here's to the rituals and giggles we share,
In each little moment, meaning's laid bare.

Frayed Edges of Reality

I found a loose thread in my tangled old sweater,
Pulling it slowly, the world couldn't be better.
A pizza delivery guy's flying with style,
As details unravel, they bring quite a smile.

Invisible ink sings from the walls of the room,
While socks whisper secrets of impending doom.
Are they mismatched due to a cosmic design?
Each with a purpose, or just mine and thine?

In kitchens where spatulas dance with delight,
And paperclip armies prepare for a fight.
They challenge my sanity, but oh what a game,
In the chaos of life, nothing's ever the same.

So here in the madness, I find a sweet thread,
A mishmash of moments, all joyfully spread.
Embrace the absurd, let the details confound,
For woven in laughter, true meaning is found.

The Dance of Minor Notes

A symphony starts with a clatter and crash,
The chaos of kitchens, a culinary splash.
Each spatula swings, as if drawn in a trance,
While flour does pirouettes in a lively dance.

A chef fights with onions, a curious clash,
Are they weeping with joy or just hoping for cash?
Boiling pots bubble, serenading their fate,
In every small blunder, we Cheshire-cat wait.

The dishcloths are gossiping, spilling the tea,
On the salad that's wilting, looking for glee.
A hint of confusion dances on the stove,
Like soufflés unsure if they should rise or rove.

In minor key chords, harmonies dwell,
Like the laughter that rises when life starts to swell.
So play on, dear friend, let the details unfurl,
In this grand kitchen symphony, we find our swirl.

Mosaic of Small Wonders

A crumb on the floor, quite a treasure,
Nibbles for ants, their guilty pleasure.
A lone sock's escape, a dramatic story,
Matches its mate in uncertain glory.

The kettle that whistles, a serenade loud,
Dances with pleasure, a kitchen crowd.
Butterflies flit, but oh, where's my chap?
Can't find my phone? It's stuck in my lap.

The cat in the sun, a lazy parade,
Chasing that shadow, a charade displayed.
A jigsaw piece under the couch is found,
It's an adventure, in chaos, profound.

A mug that cracked, now art in disguise,
Coffee drips slowly, like life's little lies.
Each little moment, a sparkle, they say,
Makes a mosaic of mundane ballet.

Glimmers in the Gloom

In the corner, a light bulb flickers,
Think it's a ghost or just caffeine snickers?
The laundry is piled like Mount Everest high,
Yet, I spy a sock that's been left to dry.

Each missing shoe tells a tale of delight,
Did they conspire to vanish from sight?
The clock ticks on, mockingly slow,
Announcing the moments, putting on a show.

Crumbs in the bed, a sweet midnight feast,
Evidence left by a midnight beast.
Laughter erupts, in the depths of despair,
These silly little things lighten the air.

Glimmers of joy in a life that feels gray,
Make a dull Tuesday feel like a play.
So embrace the chaos, let laughter ignite,
In the gloom, find the spark, and let it take flight.

Ephemeral Journeys

A leaf floats down with elegant ease,
Dresses my path like nature's tease.
Each puddle glistens, a reflective delight,
Holds the sky's secrets, if caught in the light.

The ice cream cone drops, a sticky affair,
A sad little plop, but I don't really care.
The silly hats worn at the corner café,
Remind me of whimsy that's here just to stay.

A text gone wrong plans an epic tale,
Of cats singing softly, oh, they never fail.
Each silly misstep, a playful embrace,
Makes every moment a whimsical race.

So gather your smiles, let worries take flight,
In this brief little journey, find humor tonight.
A spark of the silly in each fleeting glance,
Reminds us to laugh, to frolic, to dance.

The Poetry of the Ordinary

A burnt toast breakfast, charred to a crisp,
But buttered so lovingly, it starts to whisper.
The laundry basket full, a fabric surprise,
Each shirt with its story, no need for disguise.

Baking cookies that hilariously flop,
Yet the scent wafts through, a delicious backdrop.
Maps won't guide why socks pair so strange,
Or how every lost key seems to rearrange.

The plants in my window with a thirst for gossip,
Their leaves telling tales like some old musty script.
Life's madness circles like ducks on a pond,
In the chaos, the charm is quietly fond.

So let's toast to the normal, the mundane, the small,
For it's in these moments that we truly stand tall.
Laugh through the hustle, with hearts so sincere,
For the poetry lies where we wander and cheer.

Rediscovering the Everyday

In the toaster, crumbs dance all night,
Like tiny gremlins in a toast delight.
The coffee drips like a slow-motion show,
Each drop a laugh, a moment to grow.

Socks hide in corners, what a game!
They're building a tribe; isn't that lame?
The fridge hums a tune, proud of its role,
It's the DJ of snacks, creating patrol.

Birds argue over who gets the seat,
While the cat plots her next stealthy feat.
The world spins on, it's all quite absurd,
Revealing the laughter in the mundane world.

So raise a glass to the peanut jar,
To the marathon of distant stars!
Finding joy in the ordinary's charm,
Isn't that what keeps us warm?

Hidden Gems in the Routine

Every morning, the cereal whispers,
"Choose me for crunch, skip the drizzlers!"
Milk splashes like a mini wave,
And the spoon's a surfboard, if you're brave.

The traffic lights dance in a row,
Red, green, yellow—who's the star of the show?
Cars honk a chorus, a musical blast,
As I sip my coffee, slow but fast.

The pencil dodges paper with flair,
Writing notes like it's in mid-air.
And each typo is a pun waiting to bloom,
A giggle trapped in the office gloom.

So treasure the gems that life tends to hide,
From the polka-dots on the cat's backside.
Finding fun in the strictest routine,
Is like discovering gold where you've never been.

Whispers of Connection

A nod from a stranger, a smile that beams,
Like coffee spills mingling with dreams.
We share the pavement, a fleeting embrace,
Two souls colliding in the human race.

Text messages fall like autumn leaves,
Each one a tale that our heart believes.
A meme shared at dawn spreads the cheer,
Winking emojis, our connection is clear.

At the grocery store, carts clash and weave,
An aisle performance, we all believe.
"Oops, sorry!" echoes with laughter and grace,
In the chaos, we find our safe space.

So lift your cup to the stumbles we share,
The quirks that bind us in moments rare.
In the whispers of life, the giggles collide,
Revealing connections where happiness hides!

A Garden of Tiny Details

In the garden of socks, a mixtape thrives,
Here's a story of those who dive.
Beneath the couch, lost treasures await,
Like ancient scrolls — a colorful fate.

The clock ticks funny, counting its dreams,
Of the goofy things, or so it seems.
A dog's playful bark is a symphony grand,
Conducted by nature with a wagging hand.

Butterflies giggle while sipping on dew,
Painting the petals a rainbow hue.
And every blade of grass holds a secret so bold,
As laughter emerges in the stories they hold.

So, stroll through this garden with eyes open wide,
Find joy in the tiny, let curiosity glide.
In this patchwork of wonders, let's pause and explore,
The zany details that life has in store!

Colors in the Chaos

In a world where socks mispair,
My left foot dances with flair.
The cat wears a hat, it's quite absurd,
Chasing dust bunnies, oh how they stirred.

Spilled juice on the table—what a sight,
It splatters like art, a warm delight.
I'll call it 'Chaos'—a masterpiece,
Hang it up high, let my worries cease.

Expectations hop like a rabbit,
While plans tease me with an old habit.
I laugh at the mess life throws my way,
In every stumble, I swirl, I sway.

So here's to the quirks, the jests we weave,
In every mishap, there's joy to perceive.
With paint on my hands and giggles afloat,
Let's celebrate chaos, let's dance and gloat!

Symphonies of the Subtle

Whispers of toast with butter spread,
Under the humming of my cat's head.
A rogue crumb sings a crunchy tune,
While coffee spills like a morning moon.

The tiny ants march in parade,
Carrying crumbs—oh, what a trade!
They've got plans, while I'm still in bed,
Plotting my move for the breakfast bread.

Each tick of the clock sounds like a joke,
Rolling laughter through morning smoke.
Life's silly moments, though often missed,
Compose symphonies of an ecstatic twist.

So I'll twirl in my messy socks,
Dance with the clock, ignore the clocks.
For in each giggle, a treasure hides,
In subtleties where the humor resides.

From Fragments to Form

Like jigsaw pieces scattered around,
Twilight moments, humor's abound.
A wayward sandwich on the floor,
Best served with laughter, who could ask for more?

Each hiccup of fate brings forth a grin,
As mismatched shoes start to spin.
Transformation's dance, it's a peculiar show,
From silly to serious, how far can we go?

A pancake flips, lands on the cat,
Who out of surprise just gives me a pat.
Life stitches together the chaos we find,
From fragments of moments that tangled unwind.

So toast to the mornings where chaos reigns,
In laughter and fragments, joy still remains.
With each little quirk, we soon will realize,
The art in our mishaps is a quirky surprise.

Tidal Pools of Thought

Thoughts like shells on the sandy shore,
Washing in waves, then out they pour.
A crab in a suit, how silly it looks,
Searching for wisdom in old storybooks.

In tidal pools, reflections are funny,
A fish in a fedora, isn't it a sunny?
They dance like seaweed, twist and sway,
While I ponder what to wear today.

With laughter a splash, I skip through the tides,
Collecting the moments where humor resides.
Each bubble of thought floating by in the blue,
A message from mermaids, "Remember, be you!"

So leap with abandon, let giggles take hold,
In the ocean of thoughts, let your heart be bold.
For in every tide that rolls in with grace,
Lies the joy of existence, a light-hearted space.

Singular Hues

In a world full of colors, so bright and bold,
A toaster's dull silver just can't be sold.
Yet in morning's warm glow, it's quite the delight,
With burnt toast singing, 'I'm crispy and slight.'

The socks in my drawer, a mismatched affair,
Who knew they had secrets, this peculiar pair?
They dance in the wash, in their spin cycle craze,
Like tiny ballet stars, caught in a daze.

The cat on the windowsill, napping away,
Ignores the great dramas that humans display.
With a flick of her tail, she claims her domain,
As if pondering, 'Does this all drive them insane?'

So let's raise a glass to the quirks we might miss,
The bites of fine humor, the moments of bliss.
For the things that we overlook, like a fly on the wall,
Might just hold the secrets to the best punchline of all.

The Beauty in the Unnoticed

Underneath the couch, dust bunnies convene,
A party they throw, almost fit for a queen.
They dance with my keys and my lost rubber band,
A celebration of chaos, all perfectly planned.

The lid's always missing from my favorite jar,
Seems to have vanished, like dreams near a car.
But guess what? The ketchup's been living its best,
With no cap or no care, it's still up for a fest!

A sprinkle of sugar might brighten a pie,
Yet crumbs on my shirt tell no lie.
I laugh with each morsel that falls from my plate,
Who knew crumbs could be such a delightful fate?

So here's to the moments that slip through our gaze,
The small things that keep us in perpetual daze.
For when we stop searching for grandeur and fame,
We just might find joy in a sneeze or a name.

Shadows of Significance

The shadows stretch long as the sun dips low,
A reminder that secrets in darkness can grow.
But my shadow's been lazy, lying flat on the ground,
I think it's been binge-watching shows all around.

A plant on the sill, totally ignored,
Finding ways to survive, its existence adored.
From dust it declares, 'I'm not just a weed!'
While I scratch my head, pondering what it might need.

The clock on the wall ticks its predictable tune,
Yet today it decided to run off to noon.
As I chase after time, with a laugh and a scoff,
It retreats to its zone like, 'Please, hold on, drop off!'

A book on the shelf, it's never been read,
But its cover's so pretty, it just fills me with dread.
Still, I cherish the shine of its untouched spine,
While it whispers sweet secrets, 'Just give me some time!'

Nuances Unseen

The coffee spills over, as if in a rage,
It jumps on the counter like an unruly page.
"Oh look," cries the mug with a cheerful face,
"Caffeine ballet, we're setting the pace!"

The socks in the dryer, oh what a delightful mess,
Playing a game of hide-and-seek, I confess.
They giggle and tumble, a spin truly grand,
Only to emerge as a mismatched band.

My garden's a jungle, with weeds and delight,
Each bloom has a story, some wrong, some right.
Yet the little brown bug on the leaf, so shy,
Looks regal and proud, like, "I'm here, oh my!"

So amidst all the chaos, the unseen charms,
Lies humor that brightens with its quirky alarms.
For if we look deeper, within every fold,
We may find laughter in stories untold.

Echoes in the Mundane

A sock lost in the washing scheme,
Its travels might just be a dream.
Forgotten crumbs beneath the chair,
Are they secrets or just despair?

The microwave sings a familiar tune,
As leftovers plot to escape their doom.
The clock ticks loudly, mocking my pace,
Time's a joke, but I can't quit the race.

Coffee spills, a brown sea of woe,
Yet laughter rises; I take it slow.
In these blunders, a smirk I find,
The mundane has stories intertwined.

So here's to the things we might neglect,
The chaos, the joy, in every defect.
Each slip, each spill, a curious dance,
In the echo of life, I take my chance.

A Tapestry of Moments

A cat perched high on a dusty shelf,
Blinks at chaos like it's an elf.
A small sneeze turns to a full-blown show,
Who knew a tickle could steal the flow?

Chasing shadows, I bump into the wall,
The plants giggle, but I can't hear them call.
Washing dishes, I spot a stray thought,
Did I leave the oven on? Or was that just fraught?

Neighbors argue over how to stack chairs,
While I ponder the meaning of life's funny snares.
The world's a jester, in its grand charade,
Finding humor in paths that we've made.

Every laughter, every fumble we share,
We weave our tales with a whimsical flair.
In each little moment, we craft and we laugh,
A tapestry made of our own quirky path.

The Art of Noticing

The kettle whistles with joyous glee,
While socks converse in their own decree.
A spoon jumps out, in a bold display,
And I can't help but chuckle at their fray.

There's a twig that's fallen, a tiny parade,
As ants march about, their plans well laid.
A car honks loudly, asking the moon,
What's the point, if we'll leave way too soon?

In these moments grand and mundane,
I spot the laughter, I dance in the rain.
A hiccup of humor, a smirk in the fray,
Noticing life in a curious way.

So I raise my mug to the silly and small,
To the mischief and madness that beckon us all.
In noticing chaos, we might just find,
The art of living, laughter intertwined.

Shadows of Significance

A coffee stain, a map of my dreams,
Leading to lands of odd ice cream themes.
Used tissues clutter my knightly quest,
Each crumpled memory, a jolly jest.

Balloons escape, drifting to Mars,
While I chase my car keys to distant stars.
A flat tire, oh what a silly joke,
A ride with the cactus makes laughter evoke.

The pet goldfish gives me a hard stare,
As if he knows of my slight despair.
Every mishap, a flicker of grace,
In shadows of the mundane, I find my place.

So let's laugh at the quirks of our days,
In all the oddities, life softly plays.
For in each little misstep that we take,
Lies a treasure disguised in the mistakes.

Beneath the Surface

There's beauty in the crumbs we find,
Like last week's snack, now intertwined.
A rogue sock hides beneath the bed,
What pearls of wisdom has it spread?

A garden grows where weeds thrive best,
In the chaos lies our quirky jest.
Forgotten pens and lost receipts,
What treasures greet our clumsy feats?

The coffee spills, a playful splatter,
Whispering secrets that surely matter.
In each mishap, a giggle sparks,
Reminding us life's a series of arcs.

So dive beneath the surface, see,
The jest in what just couldn't be.
For in the messiness we live,
We find the joy that makes us give.

The Art of Subtlety

A wink, a nod, a glance askew,
In small moments, the heart feels true.
Like sneezes shared, and laughter's spark,
Subtlety dances in every quirk.

We tiptoe on the edge of fate,
With jellybeans we contemplate.
A dropped ice cream, a face of shock,
In those small blunders, we unlock.

A quick jest flits like a bright butterfly,
In mundane moments, we learn to fly.
With each detail, a comic twist,
Crafting memories we can't resist.

So embrace the minor, the offbeat cheer,
In the art of subtlety, draw near.
For lost in laughter, we often find,
The depth in what's often maligned.

Fleeting Footprints

Footprints in sand, a fleeting trace,
Waves wash away what leaves no space.
We trip over words, miss the cue,
But fallen leaves whisper secrets too.

In puddles we jump, a splash, a laugh,
The world a stage for our little gaffe.
Though time races past like a silly clown,
We gather moments, not let them drown.

A sock on the floor, a great debate,
Did it walk here or just contemplate?
In chaos we seek, try to be profound,
Yet in silliness, true love is found.

Let's celebrate each tiny fail,
Like a fish that's destined to tell a tale.
In their dance, we learn to cope,
Finding joy in the fleeting hope.

Intricate Patterns of Existence

Spaghetti curls and tangled thread,
In everyday life, such stories spread.
A cat on a keyboard, what a delight,
Turns typing to chaos, a comical sight.

The clock's ticking loud, but who really cares?
The funny faces hide in our stares.
Bananas peel with such eager flair,
Carnival laughter hangs in the air.

Buttons lost, it's a fashion maze,
Yet mismatched outfits earn us praise.
In oddities cherished, we find the map,
Life's patterns emerge from our goofy mishap.

So let's weave tales in stitches and seams,
Crafting the world out of whimsical dreams.
For in the quirks, the rich hues of fate,
We discover the joy in each twist of plate.

Between the Lines of Being

In the coffee shop line, I make my stand,
Counting the sprinkles in my overpriced brand.
Is it the espresso or the foam on my top?
Maybe it's the cake that makes my heart stop.

A sock that went missing, a shoe with a tear,
What's in the laundry? Just fluff and despair.
Does it matter if nothing comes out quite right?
It's the dance of the laundry that brings me delight.

My plants look at me with eyes full of guilt,
Their thirst is a joke on the love I have built.
Each wilted leaf tells a tale in disguise,
Perhaps they're just tired of grasping for skies.

So here we dance through these mundane times,
Chasing silly thoughts and rhythm-less rhymes.
With a wink and a nod, in the chaos we play,
Finding joy in the mess, come what may.

The Treasure in Trivial Pursuits

A pencil rolls off, and the cat gives a glance,
This heist of the paper, should I take a chance?
Rummaging through junk, I find an old spoon,
Was this once part of soup or a bubbling croon?

With each tiny moment, like socks lost in space,
I'm searching for treasures in a familiar place.
Underneath couch cushions, there's wisdom to reap,
A world of adventure in treasures we keep.

The turtle just laughed as he basked in the sun,
"You're worried about time? Well, I've just begun!"
The world seems to chuckle at our frantic journeys,
While lauding the bumbles of trivial tours.

So let's play the game, and embrace each surprise,
In the silliness found, we must open our eyes.
For in every stumble, in every small glee,
Lies the riches of living, just wait and see.

The Whisper of Small Things

The crumbs on my shirt tell a story I keep,
Of a feast with a cake that was way too deep.
Each laugh at the table, a flicker, a spark,
It's the little disruptions that light up the dark.

The cat on the windowsill drools with a grin,
As he dreams of his conquests, a world full of sin.
A wandering fly makes its impressive debut,
And suddenly life's theatre is starring in blue.

In the corner, a leaf fights the urge to drop,
While squirrels plan acorns—oh, the fun never stops!
Do the details matter, or is it the grace?
A twirl and a whirl in this fantastic race.

So grab your small moments, delight in the cheer,
For a laugh or a giggle can quell any fear.
With winks and good humor, our trinkets will cling,
In this tapestry woven, we're queens and we're kings.

Ephemeral Echoes

Amidst all the chaos, I hear something snack,
It's the jingle of coins in a small paper sack.
A penny for thoughts, but a quarter for laughs,
As we chase down the echoes of minimal gaffes.

The dog in the park, who thinks he's a star,
Chasing pigeons with zero grace, what a bizarre!
Yet every bark rings with a playful flair,
As they sync with the clouds floating up in the air.

In the thrilling ride of a runaway kite,
Is the tale that we tell what's truly polite?
Or is it the giggle that follows that flight,
A reminder that silliness dances in light?

So here's to the moments that slip through our hands,
In the spaces between, where the laughter expands.
Let's savor these echoes, like ripples in time,
For the joy lies in details, like rhythm and rhyme.

Fleeting Images

A bird flies by, then it trips,
It lands on a cake, or so it nips.
Moments flit, like a cat's quick tail,
Chasing shadows, in a crazy trail.

The toast pops up, a flighty snack,
Butter slides down, a smooth, slick track.
Like socks in the wash, they disappear,
All these mischiefs bring us cheer.

A glance, a wink, in a crowded room,
In a sea of chaos, there's always boom.
Fleeting laughter, a pastry's dance,
It's in the giggles that we find chance.

So cherish each laugh, every slip, treat,
In the chaos, there's something sweet.
The snapshots of fun, so vivid and bright,
Remind us that joy can take flight.

Lasting Impressions

A squirrel in a tux, what a sight,
Nabs a nut, then takes off in flight.
Fashion trends, they come and go,
But a critter in style steals the show.

Stains on the carpet, a child's grand art,
Beneath the chaos, beats a warm heart.
A coffee spill, a canvas spill,
Each mark a story, a quirky thrill.

Silly antics of friends in a frame,
The legends we build, yet none feel the same.
Every mishap, a treasure we keep,
In the mess of our lives, laughter runs deep.

The echoes of joy, a whimsical dance,
Binding us all in a jumbled romance.
So take that photo, embrace the quirk,
In the odd little things, our memories lurk.

The Weight of the Unseen

An elephant's weight carried on air,
Where is the lift? No one seems to care.
Invisible burdens, like socks gone rogue,
Each hidden struggle, a whimsical prog.

A spoonful of sugar for coffee's frown,
Invisible helpers, as we wander town.
A wink in the dark, a pat on the back,
Support is what keeps us steady on track.

The weight of a smile can move the heart,
While silent giggles play a big part.
Invisible threads, they weave and they bind,
A network of joy, in chaos we find.

So take a moment, breathe in the space,
Appreciate laughter, no hurry, no race.
In the unseen echoes, a truth we glean,
That joy isn't loud; it's quietly keen.

When Time Pauses

A tick and a tock, then silence ensues,
The cat takes a nap, the bird sings the blues.
In stillness, we find the moments anew,
When clocks take a break, shenanigans brew.

The coffee stands still, the mug doesn't care,
While socks on the floor hold a secret affair.
Each second, a giggle, each minute, a jest,
As time plays hooky, it's at its best.

Dancing in circles, the dog with a shoe,
Unfolding a chaos, with nothing to do.
When hours stand still, we giggle and grin,
For joy is a riddle, a mischievous spin.

So pause for a moment, just let it unfold,
Find laughter in breezes, and stories untold.
In the winks and the sighs, the world takes a breath,
And comedy reigns, more alive than the rest.

Subtle Threads of Purpose

A hat perched askew, such stylish blunders,
As socks plot a scheme, creating wild wonders.
Each little mishap, a thread in the weave,
Shows us the magic we never perceive.

A sandwich forgotten, left on the shelf,
Yet tastes like a rainbow, if we believe in ourselves.
Lost keys on the table converse with old gloves,
While socks tell tales of their lost, hidden loves.

A turned up corner in a doodled map,
Leads us to treasures from a whimsical trap.
Muffin crumbs gather, to craft a café,
In the small, silly details, we find our play.

So gather the threads that don't always align,
In quirky mischief, let laughter be fine.
For amidst all the chaos, beneath the rough cuff,
It's purpose in nonsense where we find enough.

www.ingramcontent.com/pod-product-compliance
Lightning Source LLC
Chambersburg PA
CBHW051656160426
43209CB00004B/914